SPAIN
the culture

Noa Lior and Tara Steele

A Bobbie Kalman Book
The Lands, Peoples, and Cultures Series

Crabtree Publishing Company
www.crabtreebooks.com

The Lands, Peoples, and Cultures Series

Created by Bobbie Kalman

Coordinating editor
Ellen Rodger

Production coordinator
Rosie Gowsell

Project development, photo research, and design
First Folio Resource Group, Inc.
  Erinn Banting
  Tom Dart
  Söğüt Y. Güleç
  Claire Milne
  Debbie Smith

Editing
Carolyn Black

Separations and film
Embassy Graphics

Printer
Worzalla Publishing Company

Consultants
Bredan Ara; Mike Ara; José Félix Barrio, Adviser, Ministry of Education, Culture and Sport of Spain; Isaac Hernández

Photographs
Roberto M. Arakaki/International Stock: p. 7, p. 9, p. 11 (right); Corbis/Magma Photo News Inc./Agence Presse France: p. 10; Corbis/Magma Photo News Inc./Roger Antrobus: p. 25 (left); Corbis/Magma Photo News Inc./Archivo Iconografico, SA: p. 28 (right); Corbis/Magma Photo News Inc./Arte & Immagini srl: p. 17 (right); Corbis/Magma Photo News Inc./Bettmann: p. 15 (bottom), p. 28 (left), p. 29 (left); Corbis/Magma Photo News Inc./Burstein Collection: p. 18 (bottom); Corbis/Magma Photo News Inc./Colita: p. 29 (right); Corbis/Magma Photo News Inc./Edifice: p. 3; Corbis/Magma Photo News Inc./Eye Ubiquitous: p. 6; Corbis/Magma Photo News Inc./Francis G. Mayer: p. 17 (left); Corbis/

Magma Photo News Inc./Reuters NewMedia Inc.: p. 15 (top); Corbis/Magma Photo News Inc./Gregor Schmid: p. 20 (bottom); Corbis/Magma Photo News Inc./Patrick Ward: p. 18 (bottom), p. 23 (top); Salvador Dali. Gala-Salvador Dali Foundation/SODART 2001, Corbis/Magma Photo News Inc./Francis G. Mayer: p. 19 (bottom); Donnezan/Explorer/Photo Researchers: p. 5; Georg Gerster/Photo Researchers: p. 16 (top); Beryl Goldberg: p. 12, p. 13 (right), p. 14 (left); Blaine Harrington III: p. 14 (right); Isaac Hernández/Mercury Press.com: p. 8 (right), p. 19 (top); International Stock: p. 25 (right); Noboru Komine/Photo Researchers: p. 21 (top); Victor Last/Geographical Visual Aids: title page, p. 22; Emma Lee/Life File: p. 4 (bottom), p. 11 (left), p. 27; Erich Lessing/Art Resource: p. 18 (top), p. 21 (bottom); Estate of Joan Miró/ADAGP (Paris)/SODRAC (Montreal) 2001, Corbis/Magma Photo News Inc./Francis G. Mayer: p. 20 (top); Stephen L. Saks/Photo Researchers: p. 24; Paul Thompson/International Stock: cover, p. 16 (bottom); Ulrike Welsch: p. 13 (left), p. 26; Ingrid Mårn Wood: p. 4 (top), p. 8 (left); Brian Yarvin/Photo Researchers: p. 23 (bottom)

Illustrations
Dianne Eastman: icon
Alexei Mezentsev: pp. 30–31
David Wysotski, Allure Illustrations: back cover

Cover: A girl, dressed in traditional costume, prepares to perform a flamenco dance at a festival in Toledo, in central Spain.

Title page: A family passes under a bridge decorated with mosaics during a tour of a canal in Seville, in southwestern Spain.

Icon: A flamenco guitar, which is larger than a classical guitar, appears at the head of each section.

Back cover: The Hierro giant lizard lives in nature reserves such as the Coto Doñana.

Published by
Crabtree Publishing Company

PMB 16A,
350 Fifth Avenue
Suite 3308
New York
N.Y. 10118

612 Welland Avenue
St. Catharines
Ontario, Canada
L2M 5V6

73 Lime Walk
Headington
Oxford OX3 7AD
United Kingdom

Cataloging in Publication Data
Lior, Noa.
    Spain. The culture / Noa Lior and Tara Steele.
    p. cm. -- (The lands, peoples, and cultures series)
    Includes index.
    Summary: Introduces Spain's folk music and dance, such as flamenco, its art and architecture, holidays and festivals, and religions.
    ISBN 0-7787-9366-4 (RLB) -- ISBN 0-7787-9734-1 (pbk.)
    1. Spain--Civilization--Juvenile literature. [1. Spain--Social life and customs.] I. Title: Culture. II. Steele, Tara. III. Title. IV. Series.
    DP48 .L56 2002
    946--dc21   2001047695
                                                      LC

Contents

🎸 A rich culture 🎸

Spain's exciting culture has been influenced by the many peoples who conquered the country over thousands of years. Evidence of their cultures can be seen everywhere — in the ancient ruins and castles that dot the landscape; in the art, music, and folk dances enjoyed in different regions; in the festivals, called *fiestas*, celebrated throughout the year; and in the languages spoken around the country.

(right) The ruins of a castle, which was built during the 1300s, loom high above ancient walls in Morellá, in eastern Spain. The walls were once used to defend the city from enemy attack.

(opposite) Crowds watch as a colle, *or group of people, form a* casteller, *or human tower, at a festival in Barcelona, in northeastern Spain.*

(top) Three girls play castanets at the Ferria de Abril, *a festival in Seville that celebrates the arrival of spring. To play the castanets, they clap the instrument together between their thumbs and forefingers.*

Religion

When King Ferdinand and Queen Isabella ruled Spain in the 1400s and 1500s, they decreed that all Spaniards must become Roman Catholics. People who practiced other religions, such as Islam or Judaism, were forced to change religions. If they did not, they were killed or **exiled** from the country. Today, almost 97 percent of Spain's population is Roman Catholic, although Muslims and Jews in the country now practice their religions freely.

Roman Catholicism

Roman Catholicism is one of the oldest **denominations** of Christianity. Christianity is based on the teachings of Jesus Christ, whom Christians believe is the son of God. His life story and teachings are written in the holy book called the New Testament, which is part of the Bible. In addition to **worshiping** Christ, Catholics pray to his mother, Mary, and to hundreds of holy people, called saints, through whom God is said to have performed miracles.

(top) Hundreds of pilgrims gather outside the cathedral in Santiago de Compostela.

Santiago de Compostela

Many Christians honor saints by making special journeys, called pilgrimages, to the places where they are buried. For hundreds of years, pilgrims from all over the world have visited the town of Santiago de Compostela, in northern Spain. They come to celebrate Saint James' Day on July 25. They believe that Saint James, whom Spaniards call Santiago, is buried in the town's cathedral. Saint James is Spain's patron saint, which means that he protects the country from danger.

Legend has it that just as a boat carrying Saint James' body arrived at Santiago de Compostela, a horse and rider fell into the ocean. Instead of drowning, they emerged from the sea covered in scallop shells. People believe that Saint James was responsible for this miracle. Today, as pilgrims travel thousands of miles on foot, bicycle, or horseback to Santiago de Compostela, they wear scallop shells as a reminder of the miracle. Once the pilgrims arrive at Santiago de Compostela, they visit Saint James' **tomb** and rub the neck of his statue to receive a blessing.

Romería del Rocío

Christians in Spain go on another important pilgrimage to the village of El Rocío, in southern Spain. In the 1400s, a hunter there found a statue of Mary in a tree trunk, in the marshes of the Guadalquivir River. At first, people from nearby villages journeyed once a year to see the statue. They believed that it had magical healing powers and could perform miracles. Now, almost one million pilgrims travel from all over Spain to see the statue in the church of Nuestra Señora del Rocío, or Our Lady of the Dew. They shout *"Viva la Reina de las Marismas!"* or "Hurray for the Queen of the Marshes!" Several times during the week-long festival, which is called *Romería del Rocío*, people carry Mary's statue around the village. Crowds of faithful pilgrims follow the statue and try to touch it for good luck.

Other religions

Although most Spaniards are Roman Catholics, about 300,000 Muslims live in the country. A group of Muslims called Moors came to Spain from northern Africa in 711 A.D. The Moors ruled the country for hundreds of years. Muslims follow the religion of Islam, which is based on the teachings of God, whom they call *Allah*, and his **prophet** Muhammad. These teachings are found in the holy book called the *Qur'an*, which is written in the Arabic language.

About 12,000 Jews also live in Spain. Jews first came to Spain with the Romans, who invaded the country around 200 B.C. and ruled for the next 600 years. Jews follow the teachings of their holy book, the *Torah*, which is written in the Hebrew language.

Pilgrims follow a statue of Mary on their way to the village of El Rocío. The statue is carried on an elaborately decorated cart pulled by two oxen.

Fiesta is the Spanish word for "festival" or "party." Hundreds of *fiestas* take place every year in Spain. Many *fiestas* celebrate holy days, but some are agricultural fairs or national holidays. During a *fiesta*, shops close, traffic stops, and everyone eats, sings, and dances late into the night.

Navidad

Navidad, or Christmas, celebrates the birth of Jesus Christ. Weeks before the holiday, which takes place on December 25, people set up *belenes*, or Nativity scenes. The *belenes* show the baby Jesus in the stable where he was born. Some *belenes* are set up outside with lifesize figures. There are even figures of camels carrying the three kings who brought gifts to the baby Jesus when he was born. Some people move the camels each night, so it looks as if the animals are approaching the stable!

Nochebuena

On December 24, which is called *Nochebuena* or Good Night, families gather for a huge, festive meal. Often, they eat seafood, as well as elaborate desserts such as *turrón*, made from almonds and honey, and nut-flavored *mazapán*, or **marzipan**, shaped like animals such as snakes. Afterward, many families attend a midnight church service called *Misa del Gallo*, or Mass of the Rooster. Families spend the next day, Christmas Day, with one another.

Some Spanish families devote a whole room in their home to the belén.

On Dia de los Reyes Magos, *children receive gifts such as toys, books, and games.*

Día de los Reyes Magos

While many children in Spain now receive gifts on Christmas Day from Papa Noel, it is traditional for families to exchange gifts twelve days after Christmas, on *Día de los Reyes Magos*. This day is also known as the Day of Kings or Epiphany. It celebrates the visit of the three kings to the baby Jesus. Throughout December, children write letters to the three kings, telling them what gifts they want. On January 5, the day before *Día de los Reyes Magos*, politicians, soccer players, and other local celebrities dress up as the three kings and march in parades, throwing candies into the crowds. That evening, children leave their shoes near the door of their home, along with some straw for the kings' camels to eat. They fill glasses, bowls, or even bathtubs full of water for the camels to drink. On the morning of *Día de los Reyes Magos*, the children discover the sweet treats and other presents that the kings left in their shoes.

Roscón de reyes

On *Día de los Reyes Magos*, families eat a special cake called *roscón de reyes*, which means "crown of kings." The cake is round, in the shape of a crown, and inside it is a little figure. Each child hopes that he or she will be the lucky person to get the piece of cake with the figure.

Semana Santa

Many important festivals take place in Spain during *Semana Santa*, or Holy Week, which is the week before Easter. Easter marks the death of Jesus and celebrates his resurrection, or return to life, after he was **crucified**.

During Semana Santa, religious groups called brotherhoods carry *pasos*, or floats, through the streets in a **procession**. The *pasos* have lifesize statues of Mary and Jesus surrounded by candles, palm leaves, and flowers. They show different stages of Jesus' life. Usually, between 30 and 50 people carry one *paso*. Before *Semana Santa*, they practice carrying the *paso* so that they can squeeze it through narrow streets. They march to the sound of drums and sing *saetas*, sad songs about Jesus' life. Many other people join the procession as penitents, asking God's forgiveness for their sins. The penitents wear robes and hoods, and many walk barefoot. Some carry large wooden crosses like the cross on which Jesus died.

Catholic groups carry statues of Jesus and his followers in a procession. The processions are an act of faith performed every year during **Semana Santa** *a religious festival held in Málaga, a city on the southern coast.*

The running of the bulls

Spain has many *fiestas* that honor patron saints. Every city has its own patron saint. The city of Pamplona in northern Spain celebrates its patron saint during the famous *Fiesta de San Fermín*. This holiday is also a celebration of bullfighting. The festival starts on July 7 with the *chupinazo*, a fireworks display at the city hall. Bullfights take place every afternoon for the following week.

The most exciting part of the festival is the "running of the bulls." At precisely eight o'clock each morning of the festival, six large bulls, weighing over 1,000 pounds (453 kilograms) each, are released from the Santo Domingo **corrals**. They run to the Plaza de Toros, the bullfighting ring on the other side of town. Thousands of thrill-seekers from around the world, wearing white clothes with red hats and scarves, wait in the narrow streets until the bulls stampede toward the ring. Then, they race to escape the charging animals. The run lasts only a few minutes, but the thrill lasts all day. All week long, the most common question heard in the streets is, "Are you running?"

In the last hundred years, more than a dozen runners have been killed by the bulls, while thousands more have been injured during the **Fiesta de San Fermín.**

Time for love

La Diada de Sant Jordi, or Saint George's Day, takes place on April 23. On this day, people in the northeastern city of Barcelona celebrate love. Saint George was a knight who slew a dragon as it was about to devour the king's daughter. When he stabbed the dragon with his sword, a rosebush sprouted from the dragon's blood. George plucked the most beautiful rose and gave it to the princess.

April 23 is also International Book Day. It marks the day in 1616 when two famous authors died: British author William Shakespeare and Spanish author Miguel de Cervantes. Today, celebrations for *La Diada de Sant Jordi* and International Book Day are combined. People in Barcelona attend book signings and sing love songs in public. Men give women roses, and women give men books. Over four million roses and half-a-million books are exchanged on this day.

*People look at a **ninot** of a genie from a story called "Aladdin and the Magic Lamp." It is a story about a boy who finds a magical lamp with a genie inside.*

Las Fallas de San José

The city of Valencia, on the east coast, holds an enormous party on March 19 called *Las Fallas de San José*. It is in honor of Saint Joseph, Valencia's patron saint and the patron saint of carpenters. Before the festival, Valencian carpenters and artists create large figures called *ninots* out of **papier-mâché**, wood, or wax. The *ninots* are cartoon-like sculptures of politicians and other celebrities. Most of them are several stories high. During the festival, over 300 *ninots* stand at intersections and in public squares, and people vote for their favorite one.

On the last night of the festival, called *Nit del Foc*, or Night of Fire, all the sculptures are set ablaze in huge bonfires, except for the one that received the most votes. Like spring cleaning, the burnings are a cleansing ritual, a symbol of getting rid of the old and making way for the new. The *ninot* that is not burned is displayed in the city's Museum of the Ninot.

La Tomatina

One of the most unusual *fiestas* in all of Spain is *La Tomatina*. *La Tomatina* takes place in the eastern town of Buñol. Every year, on the last Wednesday in August, the townspeople and visitors have a huge food fight! Trucks bring in over 90,000 pounds (40,824 kilograms) of tomatoes from all over Spain. Shopkeepers around the *plaza*, or main square, cover their storefronts in plastic. Then, thousands of people pelt each other with tomatoes while outdoor orchestras play music.

*During **La Tomatina**, people wear their oldest clothes, so they can throw them out when the **fiesta** is over.*

🎸 Families and their celebrations 🎸

Spaniards celebrate special family occasions with lively and festive activities. Whether they are marking the birth of a baby, a family member's saint's day, or a marriage, they gather to enjoy food, music, and fun.

Jumping over babies

Like families everywhere, Spaniards hope that their children will grow up to lead a safe and healthy life. Every year, Spaniards in the northern village of Castrillo de Murcia practice an old custom to protect their children. They place all babies born that year on a mattress in the middle of the road. A man, dressed in a special red and yellow costume, runs down the street and jumps over the mattress. Everyone in the village gathers to watch. People believe that when the jumper lands safely, it means the babies will pass safely through their lives.

A special way of naming

Spanish children's last names, or surnames, are made up of two parts. The first part is the father's surname, and the second part is the mother's surname. For example, if Marina Montoya López marries Antonio Serrat Domínguez, and the couple has a child, the child's last name will be Serrat Montoya. If the family is very proud of its ancestors, the children might have all four surnames, Serrat Montoya Dominguez López, although the child's legal last name will just be Serrat Montoya.

(top) A family gathers outside church after a first communion ceremony. At their first communion, Roman Catholic children who are seven or eight years old eat for the first time a wafer that represents the body of Christ.

Birthdays and saints' days

Spaniards sometimes name their children after saints. These children celebrate their saint's day, as well as their own birthday. For example, a child named Pedro is born November 16, but the saint for whom he is named, Saint Pedro, has his saint's day on June 29. Pedro would celebrate his birthday in November with a party and presents, and then celebrate his saint's day on June 29 by going to church. Some families have a special dinner on this day.

Spanish children have exciting birthday parties. At some, children take turns using sticks to hit a *piñata*, a brightly decorated pot or papier-mâché figure. When they hit the *piñata* hard enough, it breaks, and little toys and candies spill out. In another birthday tradition called the *tirón de orejas*, or the "pulling of the ears," party guests pull the ears of the birthday girl or boy, the *cumpleañera* or *cumpleañero*. For example, if a child is turning twelve, each guest pulls the child's ears twelve times.

After wedding ceremonies, guests often throw rice and rose petals over the bride and groom to wish them health and prosperity.

Spaniards often celebrate birthdays with cake, parties, and presents like these girls are doing at an outdoor café. Saints' days are marked privately.

Here comes the bride

Weddings in Spain are a joyous time for family and friends. Most weddings take place in a church. After the ceremony, the newly married couple and their wedding guests attend a large party that can last until six or seven in the morning. Often, the guests give the bride and groom money instead of wedding gifts. Sometimes, to raise more money for the couple, the groom's tie is chopped into pieces, and the pieces are **auctioned** to the guests. The Spanish have many other special wedding traditions. For example, the bride puts a straight pin through the jacket of each unmarried man, with the head of the pin facing down. If the pin falls off the jacket by the end of the night, it means that the man will marry soon. Every guest leaves the wedding with a small gift on which the couple's names appear, such as a small bouquet of flowers or a **ceramic** figure.

13

Music and dance

The kind of music Spaniards listen to depends on where they live. In the northwestern region of Galicia, harp and bagpipe songs echo through small fishing villages. In the south of Spain, the powerful rhythms of flamenco shake the floorboards of cafés. Radios across Spain play everything from American rock 'n' roll to reggae, rap, house, and techno music.

Instruments

Musicians in each region of Spain play different instruments. The Celts, who settled in the north around 1000 B.C., brought bagpipes, called *gaitas*, and harps, called *arpas*, from their home in northwestern Europe. These instruments create music that is powerful and often a bit sad. The Basques, who live in the north of Spain and south of France, play the *txitsu*, a kind of three-holed oboe that sounds like a flute. Musicians have played this instrument for over 25,000 years. Basques also play a lively type of music called *trikitrixa*, which means "devil's bellows," on accordions. The Moors from North Africa brought tambourines and a stringed instrument like a guitar, called a lute, to the south of Spain. People in the south of Spain also use tambourines to beat out strong, exciting rhythms. Today, Spanish musicians play many of these traditional instruments in new ways. For example, some modern CDs feature electric bagpipes.

Musicians playing **txitsus** *and drums parade through the crowded streets of Pamplona during the* **Fiesta de San Fermín.**

The guitar

People often think of the guitar when they think of Spain, partly because the instrument was created there in the 1500s. Spanish craftspeople developed two types of guitars: classical and flamenco. The flamenco guitar is larger than a classical guitar and has a much deeper, warmer sound.

Guitars and mandolins are popular instruments in Spain. Mandolins are smaller than guitars, have shorter necks, and do not have as many strings.

Famous guitar players

Many guitar players who are well known throughout the world came from Spain. They include Andrés Segovia (1893–1987), Narciso Yepes (1927–1997), and Paco de Lucía (1947–). Spanish composer Joaquín Rodrigo (1901–1999) wrote one of the few pieces of music for guitar and orchestra, the dramatic *Concierto de Aranjuez*.

Singers

Many extraordinary opera singers come from Spain, including Montserrat Caballé (1933–), Plácido Domingo (1941–), and José Carreras (1946–). Spain is known for a special kind of opera called the *zarzuela*. The *zarzuela* is a light romantic operetta that tells stories about Spanish life, using song and dance. Hundreds of Spaniards watch their favorite opera stars sing in these operettas in theaters and sometimes on television. Pop singers from Spain are also famous throughout the world, including Julio Iglesias, his son, Enrique Iglesias, and Alejandro Sanz.

Folk dance

Dance, as well as music, is an important part of life in Spain. The Basques have over 400 folk dances, some of which reflect their close ties to the land. With turns, kicks, and the striking together of sticks, Basque dancers imitate a farmer's activities. The Basques also perform exciting sword dances, where they lift other dancers over their heads. These dances are accompanied by accordions, Basque flutes, and the *txistu*.

Pablo Casals (1876–1973) was best known as a cellist, but he was also a conductor, composer, and pianist. His remarkable technique on the cello attracted many people around the world to an instrument that was not well known. He was given many awards during his lifetime.

(above) Montserrat Caballé performs at the Liceu Theater in Barcelona. Montserrat Caballé is a soprano, which means that she sings the highest parts of an opera.

Sardanas and jotas

People in Barcelona dance the *sardana* every Sunday in the *plaza* outside the cathedral, as well as at local festivals. In a big, slow-moving circle, they perform skips and jumps while holding hands. Everyone in the community joins in, from elderly people to young children. The *jota* is a faster dance, with lots of hops and twirls, that comes from Castile and Aragon, in the north. It can be danced by individuals, couples, or a whole group.

Flamenco

When Gypsies came to the south of Spain from India in the 1400s, their music mixed with the music of the Moors and Jews who lived in the region. The result was a style of music called flamenco. Some flamenco songs are full of sadness and loss, while others are lively.

Over time, flamenco also developed into a type of dramatic dance performed to the music of the flamenco guitar. In flamenco dance, both women and men click their heels and toes against the ground in intricate steps called *taconeo*. The female dancers make graceful hand movements, including *flores* or flowers, with their fingers and wrists. The male dancers' hand movements are stronger. Flamenco is accompanied by clapping, snapping, shouting, and the clicking of instruments called castanets. Castanets are pairs of small, hollow disks that are worn on the fingers.

The circle in which people dance the **sardana** *represents everyone working together. If you join the circle, you must participate in the dance even if you do not know all the steps.*

There are two main types of flamenco dances: **cantejondos**, *which are serious and full of passion, and* **alegrias**, *which are happy and lighthearted. Which type do you think these dancers are performing?*

One of Madrid's most famous sites is the Museo Nacional del Prado, or the Prado. The masterpieces in this gallery include works by Spain's greatest artists, which Spanish royal families collected throughout history. The Prado is not the only place to find art in the country. Many other galleries can be found throughout Spain. Magnificent paintings and sculptures add to the beauty of tiny rural churches scattered across the land. Impressive statues stand in village *plazas*, and elaborate tile patterns decorate the walls of houses.

Religious art

In the 1500s, the Catholic monarchs Ferdinand and Isabella ordered Spanish artists to produce paintings and sculptures with religious themes only. Most subjects in the paintings were shown in a natural, realistic way. The religious paintings of the artist El Greco (1541–1614) were different. El Greco was born on the Greek island of Crete, but did most of his work in Spain. His real name was Domenikos Theotokopoulos, but people in Spain called him El Greco, which means "The Greek." He painted people with long bodies who were often in distorted positions, making them seem tense and dramatic. El Greco was also known for painting landscapes, which were not common in Spain at the time.

Bartolomé Esteban Murillo

Another Spanish artist who painted religious scenes was Bartolomé Esteban Murillo (1617–1682). Murillo also painted scenes of everyday life, such as the young, homeless boys who begged on the streets of Seville, where he lived.

(above) One of El Greco's most famous paintings is **View of Toledo.** *This painting shows the central Spanish city of Toledo, where El Greco lived, with a stormy landscape that seems to be moving.*

Bartolomé Esteban Murillo sometimes used his beautiful wife, Beatriz, as his model for Mary, Christ's mother. Many of his paintings, such as this one called **Madonna and Child,** *show Mary holding the young Christ.*

Art of the court

Kings and queens throughout Spain's history paid artists to paint **portraits** of the royal family. When Diego Velázquez (1599–1660) was only 24 years old, he became Painter to the King. For the rest of his career, he painted realistic portraits of the royal family and other members of the king's court. He was one of the first artists to depict the dwarfs who worked in the court as entertainers with respect and sympathy.

No one is sure if, in his painting **Las Meninas** *or* **The Maids of Honor,** *Velázquez was painting the king and queen, whose reflections are in the mirror at the back of the room, or their daughter, Princess Margarita, as the king and queen were looking on.*

Francisco Goya

Francisco Goya (1746–1828) worked in King Charles III's court, painting portraits of Spanish **nobility** and historical events. His early paintings show people enjoying outdoor activities, such as picnics. In 1792, Goya caught a mysterious illness that left him deaf. After that, his work became more negative, with thick, bold strokes of dark color. His portraits of the royal family made them look unattractive, and he painted the horrors of battle in works such as *Disasters of War*, a series of 80 paintings. In the 1820s, after the death of his wife and son, Goya's work became even gloomier. He painted black **murals** on the walls of his home. Some of these paintings showed scenes of witchcraft or shocking events from Greek **mythology**. These *Black Paintings* were eventually moved to the Prado.

This painting, called **Sad Forebodings of What Is Going to Happen,** *is the first in Goya's* **Disasters of War** *series.*

*In his painting **Guernica**, Pablo Picasso depicted the horrors of the Spanish Civil War through images such as a dying horse, a woman trapped in a burning building, and a mother with her dead child.*

Cubism and Picasso

In the 1890s, a new style of painting called "cubism" became popular. An object in a cubist painting looks like it has been broken into small pieces and stuck together again. One of the inventors of cubism was painter and sculptor Pablo Picasso (1881–1973). Picasso was born in Málaga, in the south of Spain. Many people think he was the most important artist of the 20th century, and that his painting *Guernica* is one of the most significant works of art. Picasso created *Guernica* in 1937, during the **Spanish Civil War,** for a fair in Paris, France. It is a disturbing mural of a town bombed during the war.

Surrealism and Dalí

Pablo Picasso also painted in a style known as "surrealism." Surrealist paintings are based on dreams and other parts of the unconscious, which is the area of the mind that a person is not usually aware of. Surrealists sometimes show the unreal quality of dreams by painting everyday objects in unexpected ways. For example, one of the most famous paintings of the Spanish surrealist Salvador Dalí (1904–1989), *Persistence of Memory*, shows large clocks melting in the desert. Other paintings created by Dalí, such as *Apparition of Face and Fruit Dish on a Beach*, appear to change depending on what part of the painting a viewer is focusing on.

Dalí considered himself to be a genius, and he loved fame. He spent much of his later life designing a museum for himself in Figueres, in northeastern Spain, where he was born. Dalí is buried under the center stage of this extraordinary building, which is covered in huge eggs.

*Depending on how you look at it, you can see a dog or a winding road that leads into a cave in the top right corner of Salvador Dalí's painting **Apparition of Face and Fruit Dish on a Beach.***

Joan Miró

Joan Miró (1893–1989) was another famous surrealist painter. Born in Barcelona, his paintings were based on fantasy and dreams. Much of his work was humorous, with distorted animals and playful shapes and lines in vivid colors. In some of his paintings, such as *Birth of the World*, Miró applied paint wherever he wanted, then saw what shapes were created after gravity forced the paint downward. These shapes inspired him to add details to the painting, depending on how they made him feel and what they made him think of. Miró also designed ceramic murals for the walls of several important public buildings, such as Harvard University in Boston.

Antoni Tàpies

Surrealism has inspired one of Spain's most famous modern artists, Antoni Tàpies (1923–). He creates paintings and posters, as well as sculptures made from materials such as metal and concrete. One of his most famous sculptures is called *Clouds and Chair*. It is made of wire, and sits on the roof of a building in Barcelona. Originally a factory, this building is now a gallery called the Fundació Antoni Tàpies, or the Antoni Tàpies Foundation, which displays many of Tàpies's works.

In Seated Woman I, *which was painted in 1938, Miró used unusual shapes to create a picture of a woman.*

Tàpies used over 9,842 feet (3,000 meters) of steel wire to make the sculpture Clouds and Chair.

Crafts across the country

People in different regions of Spain specialize in making different crafts. Andalusia, in the south, is famous for its guitars, while fiddles are made in Cantabria, in the north. Leather shoes and bags are produced on the Balearic Islands, off the east coast. Wicker and baskets are crafted from cane in the south of Spain, and lace is made in Catalonia, in northeastern Spain.

Damascene ware

In the area around Toledo, steel or bronze objects, such as plates, boxes, knives, and especially swords and jewelry, are decorated with fine silver and gold threads. This craft is known as damascening. The Moors brought damascening to Spain. The word "damascene" comes from Damascus, an Arab city in the country of Syria, famous for this kind of work.

(right) This helmet was made in the 1500s, in the damascene style. It is decorated with fine gold threads.

(top) Flower pots, plates, and vases are among the types of ceramics made in Spain.

Ceramics

Artists in Spain make beautiful clay pottery and ceramic tiles that are decorated with Moorish designs. These designs are inspired by plants and flowers, geometric shapes, and beautiful writing. The Moors, who were Muslims, did not show people or animals in their artwork. Like other Muslims, they believed that only *Allah* can create living things.

Buildings old and new

The various peoples who conquered Spain over the centuries left remains of their **architecture** behind. The Romans constructed buildings with marble pillars and statues. The Moors built palaces and public baths with horseshoe-shaped arches, pairs of narrow windows, and white **stucco** walls. Some Spanish buildings are an unusual mix of styles because different groups of people added to them over the years.

Roman remains

The Romans were such excellent engineers and builders that sections of walls that once surrounded Roman cities still stand, and some Roman bridges are still in use. Over the city of Segovia, in central Spain, rises a huge aqueduct, which the Romans built to carry water from the nearby Frío River to the town. The aqueduct looks like a bridge. It is supported by 118 arches arranged in two layers. Amazingly, people used

the ancient aqueduct until the late 1800s. The Romans built their long-lasting structures by fitting stones very closely against one another. The fit was so precise that no **mortar** or cement, both of which crumble over time, was needed to stick the stones together.

A Roman theater and **amphitheater**, built in 24 B.C., still stand in the town of Mérida, in the southwest. Romans watched plays in the theater, which seated about 6,000 people. In the amphitheater, up to 15,000 Romans sat and watched more elaborate plays, **chariot** races, or **gladiators** fighting each other. The ampitheater was sometimes even filled with water for sea battles.

(top) Spaniards still use the Roman theater in Mérida for a summer theater festival. People have been entertained there for over 2,000 years.

Moorish architecture

The remains of Moorish castles and **mosques** exist mainly in the south of Spain, where the Moors first settled. The Moors decorated the ceilings of their buildings with delicate carvings, and their brick, stone, and marble walls with geometric patterns. Moorish buildings often had central courtyards with pools and fountains. The walls surrounding the courtyards provided much-needed shade, while the water cooled the air. Some Moorish castles and mosques can still be seen in cities such as Seville and Toledo.

The Alhambra

On a hilltop in Granada, in the south of Spain, is the Alhambra. The Alhambra is a walled town with a fortress, palace, and gardens that were built by the Moors. Construction of the fortress, the Alcazaba, began in the 800s, but was not completed until 400 years later. It has 27 towers, the tallest of which is called Torre de la Vela, or Tower of the Candle. The palace, known as the Palacios Nazaries, was built for Moorish kings in the 1200s and 1300s. It is decorated with stone columns, pretty mosaics made from ceramic tiles, and beautifully carved stucco ceilings, archways, and domes. The carvings are so delicate that they look like lace. Many fountains and pools cool the palace's patios, inner courtyards, and gardens.

A long hallway known as the Puerta del Perdón, surrounds the cathedral in Seville. The cathedral was built in the Moorish style.

*The Alhambra's name comes from the Arabic **Al Qal'a al-Hambra**, which means "the red." The first rulers of the Alcazaba gave the fortress this name because, from a distance, its walls looked red.*

Castles in Castile

About 1,000 years ago, Christians in Spain began to fight the Moors for control of the country. Both sides built hundreds of castles to protect their towns from attack. Many are in the province of Castilla-León, in northern Spain. This province takes its name from the Spanish words for castle, *castillo*, and lion, *leon*. The Castillo de Coca lies about 30 miles (45 kilometers) north of Segovia. A moat surrounding the castle helped keep **intruders** away from its stone walls and towers. One of the creepiest features of this castle is its dungeon. The prisoners entered through a door in the ceiling, breaking their legs when they fell to the ground.

La Mota is a castle near the town of Valladolid. It was built by the Moors about 800 years ago. Large walls surrounding the castle kept intruders out, and a towering prison kept prisoners in. After conquering the Moors, King Ferdinand and Queen Isabella moved into the castle and expanded it. In modern times, Spaniards used La Mota as a state prison before it became a military museum.

Modern architecture

Modern architects in Spain experiment with a variety of materials in their work, including glass, concrete, and wrought iron. Elegant brick designs, as well as colorful ceramic ornaments and stained glass windows, decorate their buildings.

Antoni Gaudí

Antoni Gaudí (1852–1926) is Spain's most famous architect. Many of the houses and buildings he designed are in Barcelona. He did not design buildings with straight lines, which were common. Instead, he copied the flowing lines in nature. For example, he imitated the spirals in snail shells when he designed spiral staircases. His archways followed the shape of the web of skin between a person's fingers. Gaudí's fascination with nature led him to put sculptures of wildlife, including a lizard covered with orange, yellow, and blue tiles, on his later buildings.

The Castillo de Coca was built in 1453. It was eventually given to the Duke of Alba, whose family still owns it today.

Sagrada Familia

Gaudí's most famous building is the Sagrada Familia, or the Church of the Holy Family, in Barcelona. It was started in 1884, and Gaudí worked on it for most of his later life. He became so obsessed with the church that he began living in it. When funds for the building ran low, he sold his own possessions to raise money. Unfortunately, Gaudí died before the church was finished. While watching the construction of the church's tower, he backed into the street and was hit and killed by a streetcar. Architects are still working to complete the church using Gaudí's sketches and models, over 100 years after it was started.

Frank Gehry made the Guggenheim Museum look like it was moving by covering it with 30,000 sheets of a silver-gray metal called titanium. The titanium reflects the sun in different ways throughout the day.

Some people in Spain think that construction on the Sagrada Familia should stop and the building should be left as it is in honor of Gaudí. Others think that Gaudí intended for many generations of artists to work on the building, all adding their own style to his original vision.

Famous buildings

One of the most striking buildings in Spain is the Andalusia pavilion created for Expo '92, a large, international fair that took place in Seville in 1992. The pavilion, which presented information about southern Spain, is a rounded blue tower that has many small windows and looks like it is leaning to one side.

The city of Bilbao, in northern Spain, is home to a masterpiece of modern architecture, the Guggenheim Museum. This art gallery, which opened in 1997, houses an international collection of modern art. It was designed by Frank Gehry, a Canadian who lives in the United States, to look like a shimmering beached whale from the outside. Inside, the Guggenheim looks like a mechanical heart. Its nineteen galleries, which are similar to the chambers of the human heart, are connected by glass elevators and suspended metal walkways.

Languages

For much of Spain's history, people in each region of the country spoke their own language. Then, in 1939, General Francisco Franco, a **dictator** who ruled the country until 1975, outlawed all languages except Castilian, the language of central Spain. Today, many people in Spain speak Castilian, along with their regional language. These languages include Catalan, Euskera, and Gallego.

Castilian

Spain's official language is Castilian. Castilians live mainly in the two central regions of Spain called Castilla-León and Castilla-La Mancha. Their language, which many people simply call Spanish, is also spoken by almost 300 million people around the world. Castilian developed from Latin, the language spoken by the ancient Romans, but it has also been influenced by Arabic, the language of the Moors. Castilian words that come from Arabic are easy to spot because they usually begin with "al." For example, the Castilian word for lunch is *almuerzo* and the Castilian word for cotton is *algodón*. Some English words come from Castilian, such as mosquito from *mosquito*, potato from *patata*, tomato from *tomate*, and tornado from *tornado*.

Catalan

More than six million people living in Catalonia, in the northeast, speak Catalan. People also speak Catalan in the area around Valencia and on the Balearic Islands. There are different versions of Catalan, depending on the region. For example, Valencians speak a version of Catalan that is mixed with Castilian, while people on the Balearic Islands speak a version that is mixed with French.

A couple reads a local newspaper in Atienza, in southern Spain. Throughout Spain, there are hundreds of local newspapers written in many languages.

Euskera

The Basques speak a language called Euskera. Euskera is not like any other language spoken in the world today, although some people think it is related to the languages of ancient India. The meanings of certain Euskeran words suggest that the language dates from **prehistoric** times. For example, the word for ceiling means "roof of cave," and the word for knife means "stone that cuts."

Gallego

About 70 percent of the three million people who live in Galicia speak Gallego, or Galician. Gallego is similar to Portuguese, which also originated in northwestern Spain. Many public signs in the region, such as signs with street names, appear only in Gallego.

Magazines and newspapers fill a newsstand in Alicante, on the east coast.

English	Castilian	Catalan	Euskera
Yes.	*Sí.*	*Si.*	*Bai.*
No.	*No.*	*No.*	*Ez.*
Hello.	*Hola.*	*Hola.*	*Kaixo.*
What is your name?	*¿Cómo se llama usted?*	*Com es diu vostè?*	*Nor zara zu?*
Good-bye.	*Adiós.*	*Adéu.*	*Agur.*
Good-bye (until later).	*Hasta luego.*	*Fins aviat* or *Ens veiem.*	*Gero arte.*
Please.	*Por favor.*	*Si us plau.*	*Mesedez.*
Thank you.	*Gracias.*	*Gràcies.*	*Ezkerrik asko.*
Excuse me.	*Perdón(e).*	*Perdoni.*	*Barkatu.*
How are you?	*¿Cómo está usted?*	*Com està?* or *Com va tot?*	*Zer moduz zaitez?*
Very well.	*Muy bien.*	*Molt bé.*	*Oso ondo.*
I don't understand.	*No entiendo.*	*No ho entenc.*	*Nik ez dut gulertzen.*

Literature

Spain's earliest literature consisted of poems, plays, and essays written by the Romans in Latin. Later, when the Moors ruled Spain, they encouraged writers to produce works in Arabic, particularly poetry. Jews who lived in Spain during this time wrote poems and books in Hebrew.

El Cid Campeador

Almost 900 years ago, Spanish entertainers wrote and sang long poems, called epics, about Christian heroes. Many of these singers, or troubadours, traveled around the country entertaining pilgrims on the road, as well as people in villages and towns. One of the first epics sung in Spanish was written around 1140 by an unknown author. It is called *El Cantar de Mío Cid*, or *The Poem of the Cid*, and it is 4,000 verses long. It tells the story of a Spanish hero, Rodrigo Díaz de Vivar (1043–1099), who fought with the Christians against the Moors, and with the Moors against the Christians. His title, El Cid Campeador, means The Lord Champion.

In this manuscript of **El Cantar de Mío Cid** *from 1344, El Cid battles with a character named Martin Gomez. El Cid won his last battle after he died. The Christians put his body on a horse, and the Moors thought he was still alive and were frightened away.*

Pedro Calderón de la Barca invented characters with good and bad traits to teach people how to behave according to the beliefs of the Catholic church. Good traits, such as kindness, were represented by kind characters, and bad traits, such as greed, were represented by evil characters.

The Golden Age of literature

Spaniards produced so many great works of literature and art in the 1500s and 1600s that this period became known as the Golden Age. Two of the most famous playwrights from this time are Felix Lope de Vega and Pedro Calderón de la Barca. Felix Lope de Vega (1562–1635) wrote almost 2,000 plays. Some people boasted that he could write a play in a single day. Many of his plays were about honor and love; others were historical plays about Spanish heroes. After Lope de Vega died, Pedro Calderón de la Barca (1600–1681) became the favorite playwright of the time. He wrote plays about love and jealousy, but is best known for his religious dramas about Catholic beliefs.

Don Quixote

The most famous Spanish novel is *El Ingenioso Hidalgo Don Quijote de la Mancha*, or *The Ingenious Gentleman Don Quixote of La Mancha*, commonly called *Don Quixote* (pronounced *don kee ho tay*). Its author, Miguel de Cervantes (1547–1616), published the humorous novel in two parts, between 1605 and 1615. It tells the story of a nobleman who, after reading too many stories about knights, believes he is a knight himself. He sets out to do good deeds and fight evil, accompanied by his faithful servant, Sancho Panza. Unfortunately, Don Quixote fights battles against giants who are really only windmills and attacks armies that are really flocks of sheep. Sancho Panza is always at his master's side to help him out of trouble.

Spanish writer Carme Riera's books have been translated into other languages, such as English, French, and German, so that people in other parts of the world can read them.

Modern writers

By the 1800s, Spaniards began to write about the problems of people in their country. Federico García Lorca (1898–1936) is one of Spain's most famous poets and playwrights. His books of poems, which include *El Romancero Gitano,* or *The Gypsy Ballads*, described the lives of Gypsies with kindness and compassion at a time when many people in southern Spain were unkind to them. The Spanish author Camilo José Cela (1916–) writes about conditions in Spain in the 1940s and 1950s. His novel *Viaje a la Alcarria*, or *Journey to the Alcarria*, describes the difficult lives of people in the countryside. Cela won the **Nobel Prize** for literature in 1989.

After the Spanish Civil War, many writers in Spain focused on depressing and violent themes. Female writers began to publish stories that described the terrible effects war had on people, especially women. By the 1980s and 1990s, some of the best-known writers in Spain were women, such as Ana María Moix and Carme Riera.

Sancho Panza tries to help his master, Don Quixote, who has just been knocked off his horse during his battle with a windmill.

Folktales

For hundreds of years, Spaniards have amused their children with folktales about animals, monsters, kings, queens, or people seeking their fortunes. The following story comes from the south of Spain, and is more than 100 years old.

The sleeping prince

Once upon a time, there was a princess named Florecita. One day, a black bird landed on Florecita's windowsill and began to sing about a sleeping prince. The prince had been put under a spell by an evil magician. Florecita asked the bird, "What can be done to break the spell?"

The bird told Florecita that the prince woke for a few minutes every year on Midsummer's Eve, the evening before the longest day of the year. To break the spell, a young maiden had to pass a black feather across his forehead, so the prince would see her sitting beside him when he awoke.

"Where does the prince sleep?" Florecita asked. "So far away, you would wear out a pair of iron shoes walking there," the bird replied as he flew away, dropping one of his black tail feathers.

Florecita tucked the feather into her pocket. Immediately, she ordered a pair of iron shoes. When they were ready, she set out to find the sleeping prince. As she walked, the iron shoes hurt her feet, but she kept going. Eventually, she arrived at a small house. She knocked on the door, and all of a sudden felt a blustering wind behind her. It was the West Wind. "I'm looking for the castle of the sleeping prince," said Florecita. "Do you know where it is?" "I don't know, but if you continue walking you will reach another cottage. There you can ask my cousin the East Wind."

Florecita thanked the West Wind and set out again. The iron shoes cut her feet, but she kept going. Eventually, she came to a cottage by a lake. As soon as she knocked on the front door, she felt a cool wind behind her. It was the East Wind. "Can you tell me how to get to the castle of the sleeping prince?" Florecita asked. "I have never seen the castle of the sleeping prince, but if you continue walking you will reach another cottage. There you can ask my cousin the North Wind."

Florecita thanked him and started walking again. The iron shoes really hurt her feet, but she continued on. After awhile, she found a snow-covered cottage. She knocked on the door, and a freezing wind answered. It was the North Wind. "The East Wind told me you would know where the castle of the sleeping prince is," Florecita explained. The North Wind smiled. "The castle is just up that mountain over there." Florecita thanked the North Wind and ran out the door, barely feeling her iron shoes.

At the end of the next day, Florecita reached the top of the mountain. She looked down to discover that she had worn out her iron shoes. There was nothing left but the laces. She found the castle and knocked several times on the door. When no one answered, she went in. Florecita was surprised by what she saw. The butlers, the maids, the cooks, even the dog and cat were all asleep. Florecita wandered from room to room until she found the prince's chamber, where he was sleeping peacefully.

She had arrived just in time. It was Midsummer's Eve. The prince would be waking soon. Florecita sat down at his bedside and watched him closely. When he began to stir, she stroked his forehead with the feather. His eyes opened, and he looked at her. The spell was broken. Florecita told the prince about the little bird, and about her long journey to his castle. The prince, who was very impressed by Florecita's courage and determination, asked her to marry him. Florecita agreed, and they lived happily ever after.

Glossary

 Index